73

Time Bomb Snooze Alarm
a collection of poetry

ᏟᏬ

by Bucky Sinister

Write Bloody Publishing
America's Independent Press

Long Beach, CA

WRITEBLOODY.COM

Sinister, Bucky.
1ˢᵗ edition.
ISBN: 978-1-935904-41-0

Interior Layout by Lea C. Deschenes
Cover Designed by Anthony Wyborny
Proofread by Jennifer Roach and Sarah Kay
Edited by Courtney Olsen
Type set in Bergamo from www.theleagueofmoveabletype.com
Printed in Tennessee, USA

Write Bloody Publishing
Long Beach, CA
Support Independent Presses
writebloody.com

To contact the author, send an email to writebloody@gmail.com

TIME BOMB SNOOZE ALARM

Time Bomb Snooze Alarm

ONE, TWO; ONE, TWO FUCK YOU.

I was first exposed to the writing of Bucky Sinister not through his poetry, but through one of his "other" books. For those unaware, he has penned two volumes that could dubiously be referred to as "self-help". Following in the stumbling foot steps of so many writers before him, Mr. Sinister used to drink prodigious amounts of alcohol and then proceed to make a royal ass of himself. I was in the middle of some chain bookstore (and a twenty-year bender of epic proportions myself) when I happened upon his first book.

That book helped me get down the road to my present state- a sober and relatively sane member of society. But it also opened up a question for me. In that book, Bucky made constant references to his poetry and how it suffered under the liquid yoke. I began to wonder about said poems, and if they were worth a shit. I picked up "All Blacked Out & Nowhere to Go" and discovered that the man could indeed write.

Ah, the all pervasive myth of the hard drinking writer/musician/ artist. Our culture is saturated with it. I certainly bought into it for far too long, resulting in a huge pile of disturbingly stained notebooks full of illegible scrawling that invariably trailed off into giant block letters reading "FUCK!".

Sinister wrote a good deal about the state of mind that brings you to the giant "FUCK!" again and again. But he ended that volume on an upbeat note. After all, you can only read so many poems ending in vomit and black eyes before you want a drink. Could he write about more than just the wreckage of his past?

The volume you hold in your hands answers that question. And the answer is: A LOT more. Yes, there are some drinking tales with bizarre occurrences. Who doesn't like a good drinking story? But you can go to any AA meeting and hear those.

What really gets me with this one is Bucky's unerring ability in each poem to take you to places he's been that I know for a fact are real. How do I know this? I've been to most of those places. For those of you not from the "underground scene" (or whatever you want to call it) this book is your ticket there. A place you can't just waltz into uninvited like your friendly neighborhood Starbuck's and soak up some faux-culture with your latte. No, this is the darker side of life where some really amazing and bright things happen from time to time. Heart breaking beauty in a corner of the county landfill.

Like Bucky says in my favorite poem in the book, "The Gray Side of the Moon":

There were no camera phones
No Flip Minos
If it was happening
and you weren't there
you missed it.

If you were there, you'll recognize it. If you weren't, this book is a great way to catch a glimpse. Enjoy.

D. Randall Blythe
Richmond, VA
2011

FOREWORD

A lot has changed for me in my life since *All Blacked Out and Nowhere to Go*, my last collection of poetry. I entered the self-help world and started performing standup comedy. There were two books about recovery from drug and alcohol addiction that are now better-known than my poetry books. I'm now a self-help author with a past in poetry and who does comedy on the side. But now with this collection, I'm back to the form that made me interested in writing and reading in the first place: poetry.

There's a link to the last two books, "Gray Side of the Moon," which hopefully I've finally addressed the loss of my roommate, Rachel. Since that time of her funeral and my last drink, I've watched a lot more friends go. It's been ten years, and while it's always sad, it's not surprising anymore. What's weird is that the ones who escaped ODs and violent crime succumbed later to diabetes and cancer. We all have to go somehow.

The new poems are a little further out of myself, I think, into the stories of other people. I'm more interested in telling other peoples' stories than my own now. Either that's a sign of maturity or I've already depleted the best stories about myself.

Standup comedy is the closest form to a street poetic that we have today. There's more true poetics in standup comedy than there is in the poetry scene, sadly. I've learned a lot in the last five years performing comedy about rhythm, timing, delivery, and word choice. Aside from the first six years of my poetry, I've never learned this much. But the poetics of standup is another essay for another time.

I tried various themes for a book that didn't work out. I tried all stories of people I knew. I tried all stories about the '90s in San Francisco. I tried to write cryptic personal ads. There were a few good ones in each batch. What you are reading, is, in a way, a greatest hits collection of all these attempts. I don't want to say the attempts failed but they didn't really succeed. These poems were my favorites that inspired me to write a whole book of poems on each subject. My greatest enjoyment in my own creativity is making rules for myself, and breaking them soon after.

I'd like to thank D. Randall Blythe specifically. He's the singer for a metal band called Lamb of God. He got into my writing and has since pushed my poetry on the rest of the metal world. I appreciate all kinds of outsider art, and hope that my books are read by kids across America who are trying to make sense of their lives by reading weird books and listening to loud music. Randall and I made it out of our small town horror lives, and so can you. Get up and never stop swinging.

I'm glad to have this, my fifth book, in ten years of sobriety. Hopefully I will have five more in the next ten. I want to continue to grow as a writer and performer and be able to be as good as some of my favorites. I hope you enjoy reading this, and my wish is that I can read it to you in person some day.

WHEN THE WALL CAME DOWN

The night the Berlin Wall came down
the bars on Haight Street filled up
with a mix of all of the neighborhood idiots:
wall-to-wall goatees eyebrow rings
black ink tats
hipsters punks goths
frat boys who smoked pot and thought Primus was rad
This crew of Belgian ravers from the hostel upstairs…

Over the jukebox
blasting Public Enemy and Jane's Addiction
I competed for the attention of a dreadlocked girl
against the best moves
of a Jaeger-shot dude
wearing a Red Hot Chili Peppers T-shirt.

One guy in the bar
wasn't having any fun.
In front of him was a beer and a shot.
He didn't touch the beer,
but did one shot after another.

Some dude who was with the Chili Peppers guy
wanted him to join the party.
"Dude, drink up, brah,
the arms race is fucking over."

That got a laugh out of the guy.

Arms race?
What the fuck do you know about arms?

"Chill out dude, let's do a shot."

Chill out?
It was arms day
at the morgue today.
You fuckers have no idea.

Every time they amputate some junky's arm,
they're supposed to keep it up to 30 days to be claimed,
so you can have it buried if you want.
But the junkies never claim them.
They literally pile up in there every month
until they're cremated.
Well the fucker who had the job before me
hadn't kept up with it.
So for eight hours today
I did nothing
but throw arms into the furnace,
but I didn't get to them all.
Guess what I get to do at work tomorrow?

I pulled the dreadlocked girl outside with me.
She was Dutch
or Swedish
or something,
I couldn't tell,
couldn't remember,
didn't care.
She wanted me to light her cigarette
but we were both
so drunk and weaving
that it wasn't going to work,
so I handed her my lighter.
I told her I would walk her home.
Right then this guy showed up.
He had tribal tats running
from under his short sleeves
down to his wrists.

Where the fuck did you go? He yelled.

I'm right here, asshole, she said back.

You better have my jacket, he warned.

She threw my Zippo at him,
yelled something in another language
and ran back into the bar.
He followed after.

I looked for the lighter
but somehow,
it was gone.

How Big Pete Found Out about God

Big Pete was caught in a race riot
in the penitentiary.

Whites coming from one direction,
Mexicans from the other,
and he was neither.

They pushed him over the tier.
He flipped upside down,
still holding to the rail,
saw burning rolls of toilet paper
zipping to the earth
like fallen angels
entering the atmosphere
and prayed for his life.

I rose up from rail,
the hand of God
on my waistband.
I turned my head
and lifting me was
the biggest blackest tranny
I'd ever seen.

That's when I knew
God was looking out for me.

segal: he doesn't c
as masculine almost
killed him yet saved
by a black tranny.

24

Wild Bill's Plan for Success

Wild Bill has a tattoo
of his own hand on his chest.

You can tell it's his hand
because the hand that is the tattoo
has the same tattoos as his hand.

Right underneath that
it says,
"Fuck you, cop."

I asked him why he got it,

he said,
This way
when I get arrested
and my hands are cuffed
I can still flip off the cops.

I said,
What if you get arrested
and you don't have your shirt off?

He said,
Bro, if I'm acting out enough
to get arrested,
I have my shirt off.

What the Dotcom Years
Did For the Drug Trade

I quit dealing speed, he told me,
the economy changed.

That's when I recognized him.
He was the former speed dealer
from the basement of the Chameleon.

I had this customer who came over,
and she left a stack of resumes
on this really nice paper.
I was using them to wrap bindles.
Then I got the idea
to make the same resume
with my own name on top.
Before you know it, I had a job.
I'm making the same money,
but I only have to work 8 hours a day.
No one calls me in the middle of the night freaking out,
I don't have to watch out for cops or nothing.

We got another round.
I took my wallet out.
He stopped me with his credit card.

Every time I think they're on to me,
I threaten to leave,
and they give me a raise.

SICK FOR LIFE

I remember your voice:
unmistakable
as your bike's rumble

sincere

You said
it was hard to pick girls up in bars
not drinking,
it didn't look right
to buy them a drink
and tell them you didn't drink yourself.

*man drink & drugs
but more prison
had to drink to pick a girl*

You went back on the beer
and five months later
you were also back
on heroin.

When you shot a load of dope
in your neck
and blew out your vocal chords
to impress a hooker,
you sentenced yourself
to a lifetime
of whispers.

anger

MISTAKEN IDENTITY

Word got around that
Buck Naked was shot
and killed
by a panhandle park pigeon feeder,
a crazy homeless man
who thought himself a
protector of pigeons.

But as the word
spread it changed;
many people heard that
it was me, not him.

For the next year
people came up to me:

Oh my god
I heard you were dead.

No, I'd say,
but next time
try to make it to the funeral.

A Show About Nothing

The sounds of Seinfeld
echo off the masonry block walls
of the psych ward.

The inpatients watch
with drooling mouths,
a Klonopin-soaked Nielsen family.

When she comes
we sit on shit colored couches
against the piss colored walls.

The cops,
she whispers,
they tried to break my arm.

Her skin
is a spill of
watercolor mustard
and India ink.

The cops
beat the shit out of me,
said I was psychotic,
that's why I get to be here
and not gen pop.

She's not psychotic
but she's not well.

Over the years
her tantrums
went from emptying her purse
throwing the contents at me in the rain
to kicking out windows of bars
with her stilettos.

We used to drink together.
There was a crowd of us:
poets, writers, filmmakers, musicians.
All of us were going somewhere
turns out it was the
psych ward
county jail
and the graveyard.

ICEMARES

1

Raf and I were telling Razor stories
and like an impish demon he appeared.
We hadn't seen him in months.

Dude, where you been?

China, he said,
then Germany,
then New York,
now here.

We knew this meant
he was up to something.
He had money
or drugs
or maybe both.
Point was
we knew
we were in for one of his adventures.

Whatcha got, Raf asked.

Something we'll have to leave here to smoke, he said.

We were in the Horseshoe.
You could smoke indoors back then,
and plenty of people in the back
smoked pot by the window.
We knew he had something good.

It's ice, he said,
it's the best shit you've ever had.

Back at my place
we needed something to smoke out of
and I happened to have a busted neon sign in the house.

It was that kind of apartment.
So we broke off a piece with a curve in it.

When it starts to smoke
hit it, Razor told me.

He held the lighter under the Pyrex.
The smoke curled up and I inhaled.
The entire rock went down my throat.
Razor laughed.

You're going to be yakked.

2

...I can kill anything,
fuck anything,
and anything else doesn't matter.
I'm Charlie Manson in Doc Martens.
I'm a time bomb with a snooze alarm.
I'm Long Dong Silver
with a pocket full of condoms
and a canteen full of lube.
I'm coming in your window
when you sleep
and leaving out the back door
when you wake.
I'm a day-walking vampire.
I'm an unwrapped mummy
looking for my hand.
I'm Frankenstein's monster
with the brain of a scholar.
I can fuck you up or get you off
and baby you will remember my motherfucking name...

3

By the time we got to the Zeitgeist
I had digested the rock.
My eyelids refused to blink.
The beer went down

like Kool Aid
and the whiskey went down
like the end of a milkshake.

I picked up this China White in Berlin,
Razor told me.
Great stuff, but I shot it all
hanging out with Jennifer in New York.
I was shooting a bag at a time
before she told me
I was only supposed to do half a bag.
No wonder it was so good, I told her.

So this whole group of
Ducati scumbags shows up
and they're pissed about something

I went over to play Virtua Cop;
Raf found me and
spilled his paranoia on me.

You know what's going on here, right?
All that China White Razor did —
he was supposed to bring it to these guys.
They gave him the money for it,
and he shot it all.

The speed is getting to you, I said,
reloading the video gun
and blasting more bad guys.

Think about it, he insisted.
He brought us along as backup.

4

…you better think twice
every time they think once,
they don't need the windows,
they listen through your radio
and watch you through your TV.

Every payphone call is taped for future reference.
They have computers listening
whenever you say "drugs" on the phone
a light goes off
and they listen in.
There's a file on you in the FBI,
they have one on everyone
with a social security number,
with all your magazine subscriptions
the merit badges you got in the boy scouts
and where you went to summer camp.
If you don't register for selective service
they flag you
and start fucking with you,
little things at first
like charging long distance phone calls
you never made to your bill.
Then they cross-reference you with others
and if too many of you get together
they set you up in a sting operation.
They mark all your money
so they know where you spend it.
They watch you from the stoplights.
All those video cameras at 7-11's
feed right into their databanks.
They can put sodium pentothal
into your Slurpee
They can kidnap you
and make it look like
you never existed...

5

Raf was right,
Razor had all his money in the ice
and all the dope long ago in his arm.
He had neither to give.
These biker junkies were pissed.
They wanted their money back.

He didn't have it.
There's one way to fix any problem
you have with a junky:
throw dope at it.
Razor bought up a round
of black tar
and they soon forgot their problems.

6

...you know what they feed to cows?
Other cows, horses sometimes.
At the slaughterhouses,
to save money
they funnel out all the blood and guts and stuff
and mix it in with the grain feed.
It's mostly protein,
keeps their strength up,
but it's weird.
It can't be good to feed them to themselves,
but that's nothing
like what they feed the pigs.
All the unclaimed bodies from the penitentiaries
go right into the trough.
It would cost the government millions every year
to cremate the dead convicts that no one wants.
The pigs don't give a shit,
if it's in a trough they eat it.
In China they have these big industrial meth houses
and the guys who work there are tweaked out;
they make them work 48 hours at a stretch,
but if some guy gets all twitchy
and falls into a vat,
they just cook him right up with it.
The sulfuric acid they use
to draw the speed out of the natural ephedrine
melts him right away.
Unless they see him fall in
they don't even know it happened

till it all comes out.
That's why some speed is pink...

7

At Raf's place,
he and I smoked more of the ice.
The bikers shot the dope
Razor bought for them.
I watched Razor shoot a load in his arm
and not miss a beat.

Hey, I'll see you later,
I have to get to the East Bay.

The door shut,
and we were left with a studio apartment
full of junky bikers on the nod.

One of the junky bikers
saw a John Ashberry book on the shelf
and mumbled some story
about how he knew him,
or went to a school where he taught,
or fucked him we couldn't tell.

Raf pulled the book off the shelf.
His wife had a ton of poetry books there.
Loudly Raf read out the poems.
After a few poems,
he announced that
he was going to read the whole book out loud.
The junkies rose and staggered away, one by one.

See, he said,
there's a use for this academic bullshit
after all.

8

…there's a little man inside my chest
and he's trying to punch his way out.
There's a smaller man inside my stomach
and he's stabbing me with an icepick.
My calves are cramping.
I have blisters on my feet.
My tongue is twice the size of my head
and if my teeth touch each other they'll break.
I can feel the tumors in my lungs,
they're getting bigger,
they're definitely heavier
than they used to be.
If I can get through today
I'll be fine
unless I broke the part of my brain
that lets me sleep…

9

On Valencia street
my stomach was a fist.
I hadn't eaten the whole time
other than the rock of ice,
which felt like it had grown spines.
I got a bowl of yogurt and granola for breakfast.
I was supposed to meet up
with a friend in the Upper Haight
to get some artwork for a flyer.
On the 33 ride,
at the turn in Diamond Heights,
I felt it come up.
It was kicking its way out of me
as I exited through the rear of the bus
and threw up on the bus shelter window.

A Japanese tourist took my picture.

12-25-99 11:55 PM

Razor and I were in the front seat
waiting for his girlfriend to come back.

These are nice apartments, I said.
How much do you think they go for?

These are the projects, he said with a laugh.

These are nice projects, I said. *Where are we?*

Marin City, he told me.
By the way, Merry Christmas.

Oh yeah, Merry Christmas.
And Happy Birthday.

DESMOND THE BARTENDER

1

I'll keep you after hours.
You can drink for free,
but I get to cut your hair.

I walked into the bar at 8 pm
with hair to my tits
and walked out
with half an inch on top.

Desmond was the kind of bartender
who kept clippers behind the bar.

2

He gave me a bourbon on the rocks
but wouldn't take my money.

You can drink for free tonight,
but you can't use your hands.
You have to use a straw.
I'm also stacking one glass
on top of another.
If the stack falls,
you have to pay.

I sucked down the first one.
Desmond quickly poured another
and stacked it on top of the old glass.

My girlfriend was in the other room,
playing pool.
She was really good
but she also had double D boobs
that hung like peaches
on a high thin branch
when she shot.

Guys would get so worked up playing against her
they'd fuck up.
No one wanted to see her leave the table anyway.

I built my stack,
Desmond balancing the new glasses just so.
At the ninth glass,
I stood on a chair to get the right angle.
The bar cheered,
someone said *Go for ten!*
My girlfriend came back around the corner.

What the fuck have you done?
I've only left you here for an hour.

The cheerleaders looked away.
What made sense only sixty minutes before
seemed impossible to explain.
I was standing on a chair
drinking from a stack of whiskey glasses.

We're going home, now, she said.
And you better be able to fuck me.

3

You can drink for free tonight.
But we just got this root beer on tap,
and no one wants any.
Every drink you have
has to have root beer in it,
and you can't get the same drink twice.

Bacardi, Jim Beam, Stoli Vanil started it off.

My girlfriend,
this one different from the pool player,
cut me off there.

Oh no, she said,
Desmond you are not getting my man fucked up.
I've heard about you.

EXTREME TIMMY

1

Extreme Timmy walked into the Sacrifice
with a net on the end of a long pole
and sat on a stool with a smile.

Knowing it would cost me a drink, I asked:
What's the net for?

Whiskey, he ordered.
I took this net into the park on Valencia,
nailed a ten dollar bill to one of the tables
and told all the bums
whoever catches me a live pigeon
gets the ten dollars.
Most of 'em fought over the net,
 but the others went for it:
the winos, the junkies, and the crackheads.
One of them caught one,
but as he was bringing it back
it flew away.

2

Extreme Timmy made a film called,
Don't Tell Em You Live In a Van
Or You Won't Get No Pussy.

3

He had a thing for throwing chairs.
He bounced one off the mirror
behind the bar at Doc's Clock
and was never allowed back.

He threw one across the street
from the Baobab to the furniture store,
and it landed on all four legs.

When dared that he couldn't do it again
he launched another that hit a guy
coming out of a doorway,
just as the cops were rolling around the corner.

He did 30 days in county jail
for assault with thrown furniture.

They told me to get in a twelve-step program,
he told us
over whiskey at the Sacrifice,
So I said *okay*
but that AA shit isn't for me,
when I get 86'd from twelve bars
that'll be my program.

A Tale of Two Frankies

I knew two guys named Frank.
Neither one of them knew each other.
one was Frankie Glitter Doll
and the other was Frank's Depression.

PART ONE: THE FIRST FRANKIE

Frankie Glitter Doll was one of those
Behind the Scenes Queens,
who knew everybody
before he or she was famous
and now no one would talk to him anymore.
The way he told it,
he gave Nirvana their first gig.

Although he watched TV with us for hours,
he pretended to never have sunk so low
as to know what was on it.
TV was very uncool then,
you had to say you didn't own one
if you wanted to fit in.

On Saturday nights,
We'd stop whatever movie we were watching
for Saturday Night Live.
Frankie always asked,
What time does it come on, anyway?
What channel is it on?
Tweaker Bob always got mad,
You ask that every fucking week Frankie,
God damn it,
how can you not know?
Frankie always used the excuse
that the channels in New York City were different,
and told the same story
about being a teenager
and watching it in the dorms at NYU,

not that he went there,
but that he was that cool
to hang out with college kids then,
because the high school kids didn't get him at all.
Sometimes there would be a new tangent
about a Richard Kern film
or Nick Zedd film
that he was in
but was cut out of or
that he had to wear a pig mask
so you couldn't recognize him,
or about some bitch
who convinced John Waters
not to cast him
over some trivial bullshit.

PART TWO: THE SECOND FRANKIE

Frank's Depression
told me he taught himself to read
from reading Henry Rollins' book,
1001 Ways to Die.

He wrote three line poems,
he told me, because
he didn't know very many words.

Metal head-head,
punk body,
like a mismatched doll.
Eyes the color of Mickey's big mouth bottles,
the black of his eyes
like broken windows
in a nighttime squat.

I knew he was in town
when frowny-face graffiti
appeared in bathrooms and on street corners.

Frank's Depression
was really in love
with this one woman
and she broke his heart.
He hopped trains to be with her,
hitchhiked to be with her,
always found her.
She told me later
that's why they were together for so long.
Every time she'd bail, he'd show up.

Both Franks came to my bar.
Both came to poetry night.
Frank's Depression came to read.
Frankie Glitter Doll came
to heckle the ugly boys
and to tell the beautiful boys
that he could make them famous,
just like he did for Kurt Cobain.

Over time
Frankie laughed less
and threw more tantrums.
It wasn't impending death that bothered him so much,
it was the fact
that he would never be as famous
as he pretended to be,
and death,
coming from the other end of his timeline
to meet him halfway,
cheated him of his notoriety.
AIDS burned off his life expectancy
like smoke lifting itself from tin foil.

Frank's Depression
popped in and out of town over the years,
each time with less teeth
and once with missing no eyebrows
that refused to grow back.
His metal hair gave way

to a haphazard Mohawk
the color of a trash can in the park.
His skin became the color of concrete.
One night he got into a fight
with a bouncer in New York City
who didn't want him selling his zines
in front of the bar.
He slept it off forever back at the squat.
They called it exposure to the elements.

I have to tell you all this,
because I saw both of their ghosts
in the same week, years after they died.
I was on a number of drugs,
coming on to some,
peaking on others,
and coming down from the rest.
I told other people.
They said
it was the wind
playing tricks on me,
or that I should
lay off the booze and drugs,
or that I should
sleep more.

Frankie Glitter Doll
was heckling in my old bar,
he was in the back,
throwing a tantrum
that no one but me could hear.
I didn't go back in there for a while,
but once when I was walking past the bar
Frank's Depression followed behind me,
telling me how he likes it where he is now,
that he has a magic forty that's always full
and a bindle of speed that never empties,
but that he can't make zines
because he can't find a photocopier.

This neighborhood is full of spirits,
if you pay attention
you'll notice.

On a quiet night
you can hear the ghosts
of the SF Hags
on phantom skateboards
rolling down Capp Street,
tweaking on armshot crank,
too wired to know they're dead.

In the squats
the old junkies
tell the young ones
by the lights of candles
stuck into the mouths of forty bottles
that if they don't clean their needles,
the limbless ghost of Greenpeace Ray
is gonna come get their arms.

Out on Valencia Street
Omer stops playing guitar
to yell at someone
you can't see,
but it doesn't mean
nobody's there.

Maybe that's who
the Redman is talking to.
Maybe that's who
tells Swan what to write on his zines,
and maybe
they can hear this poem too.

Such a Heavenly Way to Die

I had a mouthful of donut
coming out of Hunt's
and coming down off acid.

This matte black Monte Carlo
stripped of its trim,
blowing smoke out its tailpipe
like a basehead on payday
pulled up and I heard,
The Queen Is Dead —
the Smiths album I had to pretend to like
when I was in an art major's dorm room
trying to make out with her.

The car was full of vatos
singing a Spanglish version of,
There is a Light That Never Goes Out.

I nearly lost my shit,
started laughing,
then they all got out,
eyelids so low
they had to lean their heads back
to look at me.
I stopped laughing.
What was left of the acid
lighting my up my fear strobes fear in strobes.

One of them started talking to me,
the others went into Hunt's.
I couldn't understand him,
not sure if he was speaking
Spanish or English,
both of us fucked up.
He wasn't speaking right
and I wasn't hearing right.

Finally it became clear:
I could hear him say,
I said,
Why you got a picture of yourself
on your shirt?

He had me there.
I looked down.
I said,
Dude, that's not me,
that's Charles Manson.

YESTERDAY'S VATOS

Back when there were pay phones
the vatos used to post up
wearing pagers
like a big FUCK YOU badge,
white shirt, black pants,
Nike Cortez shoes,
with Virgin de Guadalupe tats,
and their hair was perfect.

The payphones are gone now
like the buck ninety eight rice and bean burritos,
and I see their sons out here
eighteen years later.

Driving by in Honda Civics
hanging out outside McDonalds
in throwback jerseys,
And 1 sneakers,
making cell phone calls,
saying *dude* more than I do.
If they still speak Spanglish
I never hear it.

The virgin is no longer on their forearms,
Tupac and his cross took her place.

THE GRAY SIDE OF THE MOON

1

Dorothy walks into Rainbow Grocery
wearing her ruby red Doc Martens.

I'm looking for the good witch,
she yells out.

Everyone
raises her hand
or points to someone.

2

I watched The Wizard of Oz on a black and white TV when I was young.
I had no idea Dorothy's world became color once she landed in Oz.

It was long before we people like us had VCRs.
Either you watched it when it came on once a year,
or you missed it.

3

At the age of fifteen,
I knew what Uzi fire sounded like,
but I had no idea what it was like to kiss a girl.

There was a weird window of time in the '80s
when the gangs were better armed than the cops.
The fistfights stopped and the shootouts began.
Breakdancers traded in linoleum squares
for crack corners,
the windmills and headspins
gave way to jump-ins and drive-bys.

Crack
turned the streets
into a pinball game of teenagers running for cover.
Glass broke and people screamed

like the city went on multiball mode.
You wouldn't always see who was shooting,
you just ran in the direction everyone else did.

I hid where I could,
behind cars and trash cans,
running into the subway when it was close.

I wanted out.
I wanted to leave Boston,
go back home to Arkansas
where my friends
were building hot rods one piece at a time,
and dating girls who liked fast cars and drank wine coolers.

When you're a teenager,
it's easy to feel like you're going to die a virgin.
But during that time of my life,
I was really worried about the dying part.

4

I made it back to Arkansas.
I was shell-shocked
from years of street evangelism
and the violence that came with it.
None of it made sense anymore.

I quit the church for the trailer park.
Someone made me a Jack and Coke.
I looked in the red plastic cup
and saw a tornado.

5

I heard *Dark Side of the Moon*
for the first time on cassette.
Same goes for *The Wall* and
Wish You Were Here.

Later the first guy I knew with a CD player had a copy of *Animals*,
and I listened to it for the first time coming down from an acid trip,
alone in his living room while he fucked his girlfriend down the hall.

I couldn't tell if it was their sounds
or the sounds on the album
or the sounds in my head,
and I'm still not sure.

6

They say
if you put on a DVD of *The Wizard of Oz* and turn the sound down,
and put on a CD of *Dark Side of the Moon* at the same time,
they totally sync up.

They say
that if you look in the trees in the enchanted forest,
you can see one of the stagehands
who hung himself from the one of the prop trees.

They say
that Buddy Ebsen was supposed to be the tin man,
but he was allergic to the makeup.

They say
if you tattoo your face
you automatically get a GA check.

They say
if you smoke heroin instead of shooting it
you won't get a habit.

They say
live fast die young,
leave a good looking corpse.

7

The tornado set me down in California,
a world of color compared to my monotone childhood.

Jr. College was grad school for young drug addicts,
an accelerated program for learning multiple ways of getting fucked up.

I balanced my time between cocaine, mushrooms, LSD, and 100 proof vodka.
At the end of the semester I got my grades from the school in the mail.
I had forgotten about that part,
the whole going-to-class thing.

I found poets
who shot dope in the bathrooms,
smoked speed in the alley,
and smoked pot like it was legal.

They were brilliant sometimes:
brokedown angels
beatdown revolutionaries
scarfaced prom queens
glass pipe prophets
quicktounged hustlers
slowmouthed drunks

When I heard a good poem,
color came to my life briefly.

There were no camera phones,
no Flip Minos.
If it was happening
and you weren't there,
you missed it.

Fuck Dorothy for wanting to go home.
Why did she want to go back to her black and white world?
What was she going back to?
She found the land of color and wanted out right away.
The tornado was what saved me.

Laying in my bed
coming down off coke,
my heart beating like a bat's wing trapped inside me,

the euphoria gone,
I comforted myself in the idea
that I was too far from home to go back.

8

Every summer,
the American Tornado dropped Dorothies into San Francisco.
We were the unwashed and faded-gray version of the Lollipop Guild,
greeting them upon arrival.

This is for the little girl
who would rather have a meth problem
than a weight problem.

This is for the little boy
who tattooed his face
so no one would touch him that way anymore.

This is for every little boy and girl
who stood between home and a tornado,
weighed the options,
and took a chance on the twister.

9

AIDs took the first friends I made,
in a synchronized fashion,
one after the other,
diving into nowhere like Busby Berkeley swimmers.
From there it was a variety show of ODs, suicides, and freak accidents.

10

The lion wanted courage.
The scarecrow wanted a brain.
The tin man wanted a heart.

Rachel wanted fake tits.
People gave her shit
like it was different from the tattoos
and the piercings everyone else got.

They were perfect.
The wizard knew what he was doing
when he slipped those in.

I never met a lion,
but I met a kid with cat whiskers tattooed on his face.

I never met a scarecrow,
but I met people who shot speed and talked conspiracy all night.

I never met a tin man,
but I saw junkies frozen mid-walk in a statue nod.

11

Fake Tit Haiku #1

I don't care they're fake
Whoever made them: brilliant!
Fake or not, awesome

Fake Tit Haiku #2

I loved your fake tits
fake or real they are still tits
who does not love tits?

Fake Tit Haiku #3

Silicone fakies
Saline packets too fancy
I'll take frozen pea bags

12

The room spun above me.
I was back in the tornado,
spun by the winds of whiskey and bad decisions.

Above me
I could see the bottom of the bottle through the glass of the coffee table top.
All the bourbon that remained was one halo mockingly over my head.

The store was about to close and I was out of liquor.

Too drunk to stand up
but not drunk enough
to stop giving a shit.

I lost my faith in whiskey right then,
the same way I stopped believing in God on that hot night in Arkansas.
There would never be enough whiskey in the bottle again.
A river wouldn't satisfy me.

I was no longer going anywhere or from anywhere.
It was just me and the swirl.

13

Rachel told me to leave the house

Go somewhere and dry out.

I trusted her.
I trusted those fake tits.
They were at once
a lie and the truth.
A perfect duality.

14

The house fell on Rachel.
She caught strep throat,
it turned into a staph infection, and she was dead three days later.

It was Rachel died two weeks after I had left the punk house.
At her services,
pinhole-pupiled punks,
staggering drunks, and
bong-ripped mourners
stumbled past to give respects.

I held out for a while,
went to my favorite bar.
I said make it be tomorrow
and drank glass after glass of twister-drinks
one last time.

15

The first AA meeting I went to
I saw all these people from my past.
You were there
and you were there
and you and you and you.

16

Dorothy's sick,
kicking dope by candlelight
in the squat.

Her arms
are a mess of pick-marks
and homemade tattoos.
An abscess stands in the crook of her arm
like a leaning barn by the side of the road.
She wants to get it checked out
but is afraid they'll amputate it.

She holds Toto close and cries,
I just want to get back to Kansas.

Cat-Whisker-Face looks up from his guitar.
Shit, girl, he says,
you're on the wrong side of Portrero Hill.

TRUST IS A LUXURY

Two of my coworkers are fucking.
They think no one knows.

They come in to work,
one takes the stairs
and the other the elevator.

They take long lunches together but
say nothing to each other in the office.

I want to tell them it's okay,
I don't care,
no one cares.

It wasn't too long ago
that people used to fuck at work.
Fucking off meant just that:
you'd fuck off in the supply closet,
or an empty conference room,
or the stairwell that no one uses.

Now fucking off
means being on the Internet or
texting someone from your cell.

Even in the dotcom days
there were drunken company lunches,
baristas who sold grams of coke and eighths of weed
to anyone needing to take the edge off.
Not much fucking but there was plenty of porn.
A little more than ten years later
it all sounds made up.

★★★

It's a beautiful day in Marin County
and if there weren't a prison here,
I couldn't afford to stand on this property.

At San Quentin
there's a gun tower
between you and God.
Pray all you want,
but if you run
you will be shot
on general principle.

The sky is
low on the yard:
starts one breath
above the tower,

San Quentin
is a small island
surrounded by
the ocean of not here.

From the time the outer gate closes
until I get to receiving,
I think about every stupid thing
I could've gotten caught for,
How this would be a lot worse
than volunteering to run a poetry workshop.

I want to thank you for coming in,
she tells me.
We don't get a lot of volunteers in here.
This is the hardest class to get into.
Everyone's really excited about coming here.
There's just one thing —
you have to sign this waiver,
we have a no hostage policy here.
If you are abducted during your class
we will not negotiate for your release.
It's just a formality.

And I think,
No, it's not.

One more thing,
she says.
Here's a whistle —
if anyone gets weird,
just blow this and we'll be on it.

***

In a big meeting my boss says,
Well that's all water over the dam now.

I start to laugh and cover it with a fake cough
and throat clearing.

That's not the expression.
Water under a bridge is normal.
Water over a dam is very bad.
That's a disaster.
Everyone is going to die.

I know how to do my work,
but I don't know how to behave in an office.

The only job that ever came naturally to me
was working in a bar,
bouncing, barbacking, working the door;
it all made sense to me.

I understand how to break up a bar fight,
but not how to participate in a conference call.

This job is fine
until there are other people around.

The boss says,
We're not drinking the Kool Aid on that one.

It's a reference to the mass suicide at Jonestown.
and he's talking about a corporate policy
on office supplies.

In the sexual harassment seminar
I was required to take,
they said I wasn't allowed to say anything
that was offensive to anyone else,
even if it was on accident.
After 45 minutes of explaining it,
and a half hour video,
they said,
Just keep the golden rule in mind.

Which doesn't apply —
if I treat people like I want to be treated
I'll be fired.

***

At San Quentin
they tell me,

*Don't ask anyone
what he's in there for.*

*Don't give out your address
or your phone number.*

*Don't give anyone
any articles of clothing.*

*And if you run on the yard
you will be shot —
if something happens
lie face down on the ground.*

***

At work
they put up hand sanitizers everywhere.

I think,
*Who the fuck
will use this?*

But people complain
that they empty too fast.

There's an extra trash can
by the bathroom door
so people can throw away
the paper towel they use
to open the door.

I have gone to neighborhoods
I shouldn't have been in,
bought stuff I was pretty sure was drugs
from people I didn't know,
and smoked them
with a pipe I made from garbage,

and I'm fine.

Raw chicken, old mayonnaise,
rusty nails in the foot —
there are germs to be wary of
but it's not the germs on your keyboard
that are going to take you out.

***

In San Quentin
loose tobacco is currency
and trust is the luxury of free men.

There's a guy
I think is mad dogging me
the whole first class.
A little while later
I find out
he's just missing an eye.

One guy says
all he does
is eat sleep shit
work out and write poems

and jerk off
and I think
that's what I call Saturday.

Another guy talks about his teeth.
Neither of us had gotten dental care
until the year he went to prison.
and I started working an office job

One guy tells me
he hasn't been home for a family vacation
in five years.

That sounds great I think,
a perfect excuse.

★★★

For most of my life
I thought the office job
was impossible for me.
I thought San Quentin was more likely.

I have more friends who have done time
than have had corporate jobs.

I've heard more stories
about cellmates
than CEOs.

I read poems to the convicts.
They laughed in the right places,
got quiet in the right places,
they understood what I was saying.
I knew how to talk to them.

At work I agonize over emails,
don't want them to be taken the wrong way.
I'm afraid of offending people,
sounding snide or sarcastic,
or that I don't give a shit,

especially when I really
don't give a shit.

The convicts know what it's like
to hurt someone and feel bad about it,
that losing a fight heals,
but winning one can haunt you.
Free or convicted,
none of us really gets away
with anything.

In the '90s I was temping.
Fight Club came out.
We were talking about it,
I said, *How the hell would you find*
that many guys who had never been in a fight before?
The room was quiet.
I was the only one.
It totally ruined my next
ecstasy trip
I was in the Cat Club.
They were playing T Rex:
70s music 80s clothes and 90s drugs.
I was almost thirty,
still figuring out why
my life wasn't normal.
Until then I thought it
was just me.
I thought
there was just something
wrong with my brain
that I couldn't take it
I tried to tell this girl
who looked like David Bowie.
I said, *We are all normal,*
it's just our lives that are fucked up.
She looked at me and smiled,
pointed to her ear and mouthed,
I can't hear you.

The convicts know what it's like
to be small
and have to protect yourself
the best you can.
That fear and small
are forever connected.
They know what drugs make you feel big,
and that big means not afraid.

★★★

The workshop was only two weeks long.

I went back to work.
One of my coworkers accidentally
forwarded an email to me.
He was talking mad shit.

Bar life
Drug life
Says I have to call him out
in front of everyone.
Don't look like a punk

But I wasn't in a bar
or a crack house.
This wasn't a drug deal,
this was an office
at the end of the F Line
at a job that
bought me a condo,
a truck,
and got my teeth fixed.

I printed the email out and took it to HR,
filed a harassment complaint.
There were a bunch of meetings after that.
I never felt any better about it.

I went home,
worked out,
wrote a poem,
ate,
shit,
jerked off,
and went to sleep.

The Pug and I Miss You. Come Home.
(A Love Poem for the Zombiegeddon)

1

It was supposed to be simple:
you were going on tour,
leaving the pug with me,
and you would be back in two months.

Then came the zombies.

It was horrible,
like we always imagined,
as the movies and comic books predicted,
but eventually it was over.

In the span of weeks,
the whole world became complicated.
You were supposed to be back a week ago.
I don't know if you're late
or not coming.

Waiting is worse than a zombie attack.

2

I walk the pug several times a day,
still carrying a shotgun and a propane torch,
just in case.

After the zombies finally gave out and died,
Oakland was filled with flies like you wouldn't believe.
The flies were followed by the frogs and birds.

The smell is overwhelming:
rotten zombies and birdshit.

The pug doesn't seem to mind.
In fact, he seems to be cataloguing all the bodies

for some kind of doggie smell diary.

The pug and I go around the lake, usually,
where I've burned most of the bodies but there's a stench
coming off the lake that I don't know how to fix.

The heartbreaking part is when we get home,
he always looks to see if you're there.

3

When the shit was going down,
I was conscripted into the military,
when they came through and found out I could shoot.
There's always room in the army
for a country boy
who's good with a rifle.

When they pulled out,
they let me keep the M24 Remington.

I camped out with the pug
on the roof of the building
across from Mama Buzz
and shot the last remaining
hipster zombies
as they straggled
with their vestigial memories
for a cup of coffee.

That's when I saw the ex,
the one who told me
she was moving to Portland
and never did.

Through the scope,
I watched her lope up the sidewalk
with her feather earrings,
art portfolio under her arm.
I took the shot.
Closure.

4

If you're reading this,
come down to the Tribune building.
That's where we live now.

I hope the two stops of the tour
were good for you.

I hope you sold a lot of books.
The world needs books
now more than ever.

Fuck, I hope you're alive.
The pug believes you are,
and I trust him.

How to Piss Off a Canadian

When I wake up, you're still driving.

It's dark out,
and much colder
than it was this morning.

"We're stopping here for Krispy Kreme donuts.
I'm going to see what the big deal is," you tell me.

The truckstop is full of surrendered and over-caffeinated rednecks.
All the snowglobes remind me of The Truman Show.

You return with a half-eaten chocolate ring. You look pissed.

You don't say a word until you get back in the car.

"Timmy Horton's makes a far superior donut."

When you turn out of the truck stop,
you floor it
and steer us toward Canada.

THE KIND OF LOVE POEM YOU CAN'T
GIVE TO THE PERSON YOU WROTE IT FOR

What is it about your uneven teeth?
It's your only facial imperfection,
but it's what draws me to you,
it's your hottest quality.

I can't tell you,
because I know you're sensitive,
but whenever you talk about getting them fixed,
I think it would break your good looks.

It's hard to see them.
You keep your lips over them.
I have to really make you smile,
really get you to laugh to get you to accidentally to expose them.

I can't explain it,
I know you hate them,
but it's those crooked wild-west saloon shutters
that makes me want you.

UNIDENTIFIED LOVE POEM

Over dinner, you tell me
about your hard day at work in the lab.
It's rough hearing all about the lower half of a corpse found in the bay,
but I've grown used to your tales of forensic glory.

Tonight, we're going to see the new Werner Herzog film at the Embarcadero.

I'm going to like it, well,
because I have a big man-crush
on that rascally German.

You: maybe you will,
maybe you won't,
but I put up with all your girly crap films
about shoes,
closets,
kitchens, and
time-traveling mysterious men with dreamy eyes,
so you don't mind.

The Small Hours

Oakland

The boxer calls me,
asks me if I want to see her
beat the shit out of a girl from San Jose.
Fuck yes, I say.

She can't have sex a week before the fight.
She tells me she needs it tonight
good enough not to need it for a week.

She sweats
like only boxers sweat,
a complete release of fluids.

Drops fall from her chin and nose onto me.
I grab her hips, like trying to grab a catfish in a boat.
Her body is one muscle that contracts and relaxes.
Sweat rivers run down her abs
that look like two snakes
fighting their way out of Saran Wrap.

I slap those abs like I'm jumping in a puddle.
Her eyes change into a game of truth or dare.
Is that all you got?
I slap her again.
No, hit me like you mean it, bitch.
It's on, I'm full-on punching her,
I can't get good leverage from below,
but I'm giving it all I have.
She clenches her stomach muscles
in defiance.

I want to be in love with her but I'm not.
I wish I was.
I wish I could flip a switch.
She has everything I need to be in love with her,
she's tough,

but she's very sweet and caring at the same time,
but it's not love.

The feeling is mutual.
We both know that this isn't the real fight.
We're sparring partners.
I wonder if the part of me that falls in love is broken.

A few months before,
M broke me bad,
busted my heart with hers
like a monkey busting open a coconut
with another coconut.

It's the same problem I usually have
in relationships
the fucking is good
but there's so many other things that go wrong

There's listening
and thoughtfulness
and patience and tolerance,
and whatever's wrong with my brain
makes my emotional state
like a Ferris wheel
going rogue,
breaking free of the carnival
and rolling down
the streets of my relationships,
stampeding and squashing
anyone in the way.

Eventually we stop fucking
long enough
to let me say something wrong.
to forget the wrong thing
to not pay attention in a crucial moment
to fire off a word of anger with no warning

And then I hear the speech again,
the, *I think you're really great*
and have a lot of good qualities
but you have something
you have to work through
talk,
and if it's bad enough it's the,
What the fuck is wrong with you?
talk.

Portland

Nine months later,
I wake up in Portland.

Sleeping is like drowning.
When I come out of the water
I try to catch my breath,
figure out where I am.
I don't remember anything right away
and wait for the pieces to sort themselves out.

I'm with a woman I barely know,
she's sleeping in the crook of my arm.

It takes a moment for my brain to locate.
Her hair feels like the boxer's hair,
for a moment I'm not sure where I am.

Then I remember.
It comes back to me,
she took me for a donut,
we bought two,
ate the first one in her car,
and she said
we could finish the other one at her place.

She didn't want to have sex,
she just didn't want to be alone,
which was exactly my problem,
so we went to her place.

She told me stories about doing coke with Sean Penn
until I fell asleep with her on me.

It's hard for me to sleep with someone else sober,
physically touch someone at night.

I used to drink for it,
but I don't anymore.

M was the last one I could sleep with like that,
she pulled my arm over her shoulder at night
like an illustration of a judo throw.
I could believe that I would be in love again,
but I get really worried that I can't sleep with another person.

I had just had one nightmare,
which always come in a series.
There were more coming, and the next night
it would be even worse, but

my mustache still smelled like chocolate,
this girl's bookshelf was full of Bukowski and Klosterman,
not a single Tom Robbins or David Sedaris;
I knew I would be okay.
I pulled her tighter
till the heat woofted from under the blanket and across my face.

Oakland

The boxer says the other girl
might be running the lake tomorrow,
What if I run into her?
I said it will be like
Matthew Modine running into Shute
in Vision Quest.
She says she hasn't seen it.
So we watch it.
In the movie they say
life is what happens in those six minutes.

The fight is in a small gym,
an industrial space,
like where we used to have punk shows.
There are boxers of all sizes and ages,
entire Mexican families arriving
like it's the school Christmas pageant.
Old boxers from the neighborhood
shuffle around,
give unasked for advice,
tell stories that fit in the spaces where teeth used to go.

The boxer takes her turn,
and she's giving it good.
I get excited when she lands one,
I can taste the hits in my throat,
and when she takes one
I feel the vibrations in my feet.
I want to yell her name
but I'm afraid I'll throw up.

She gets hit in the gut—
I wonder if she's thinking about fucking me.

There's something about her
landing a combination that really gets me excited.
I want to rip out my stomach
and wave it over my head
like it's a soccer player's shirt.

Three rounds, six minutes, is all it takes.
She wins the fight. I want every day to be like this one.
I go outside with Adrienne and we smoke.
We're both doing a really shitty job of quitting.
We're quitting the way
that you party really hard
the night before you go to rehab.
We're smoking more than we ever have,
trying to get sick of it or something
but we're gluttons for punishment.

Boston

It started
when I got jumped at fifteen,
my first real street fight—
me against what looked like a dozen pairs of
Converse Weapons
and Adidas shell toes.
I tried to stand up but they kept kicking me.

There's a moment when the whole screen shifts to the left
and everything goes quiet.
I've been kicked in the ear and go down,
but it feels like I can't quit falling,
I hit the ground but it feels like
I've been dropped out of a plane.

The feet go away and
someone's pulling me up.
I think it's God,
but it's a Boston cop.
I try to tell him what happened
but my mouth doesn't work right,
it just squeaks out something.
My throat is huge and filled with spit.
I try to tell him I didn't see who it was and he just says,

Go home faggot.

After that my ears rang forever;
my right ear still is shit.

I lost counts of the fights
after that
One day
I got punched in the face and it didn't hurt,
it just made me mad.

The last time I got rat packed,
instead of getting up,
I hooked a guy's leg,

pulled him down to the ground,
got on top of him —
his face red as the cobblestone
I pushed it on,
and he was yelling,
Get off me!
They were kicking at me
but hitting him half the time.
I don't remember how that one ended,
the memory just stops there:
me and him stuck together.

There's something wrong with me,
there's a name for it,
but I didn't know for a long time,
I just thought it was the way I was made.

St. Louis

In 1988 in St. Louis
These two rednecks were laughing at me
so I walked across the parking lot
and blasted one of them in the face.
There was blood coming out of his nose.
He was scared.
his friend said, *What the fuck what the fuck!*
I realized they weren't laughing at me,
they were laughing at anything else.
They hadn't seen me.
I just wanted to get the first punch for once,
What the fuck, he said, *What's your problem?*

I knew I had a problem
but I didn't know the name for it,
that would come four or five years later when
someone gave it a name
but they couldn't do anything about it.

I walked out of that parking lot.
I had to walk home.

I didn't have a car.
I blamed St. Louis and said
when I got to California it'd be different—
I'd fit in.
California was fucking cool,
not like this place.
There were punks there,
and the best bands ever,
and no one would notice
that there was anything wrong with me…

M said
I wasn't right for her,
that I had anger issues.
It's the one thing I can't tolerate,
she said,
Dating you is like dating the guy in the movie, Shine.

It fucking hurts.
I can make myself smarter than anyone else,
I can read more and learn more,
but I can't fix what's broken in my head.

They cont. to be fighting violence & use as a way to be a man, but eats them alive.

Portland

There's something wrong with me,
there's a name for it
but there's no fucking cure.
There's whiskey and cocaine
but there's no fucking cure.
And I can't have whiskey and cocaine anymore,
so now I have to live with it,
and I dream about it,
and wake up from it,
and I look over
and I struggle to pull Portland's name out of my memory.
I find it
whisper, *Thank you.*
and go back under

There are chunks of time when it's all okay,
small moments like
when some hours are shorter than others
I think I can make it work,
when I think,
This time it won't fall apart.
Maybe I'm better enough;
There's still something wrong with me,
but not as bad as it was.
Maybe now I'm good enough for someone else
to put up with.
I won't hear the word crazy or insane or mental
instead it will just be quirky unique special eccentric.
I wish I were eccentric,
I would love to be that guy,
I would love to climb down the mental ladder
to the rungs where
the guy who wears a leather vest
and an iguana on his shoulder lives,
but I'm way above him,
looking up at the butthole of the guy
who just yells FUCK over and over
at the air.
That would be a good gig.
I wish I'd thought of that.
It's got to be better than my office job.

Oakland

Right after the fight
the boxer is off her diet restriction.
I need some ice cream,
she tells me.

We walk down Piedmont Avenue,
toward Fenton's Creamery.
Everyone looks at her,
sees her black eye, then looks back at me.

Asshole, their stares say. *You monster…*

ONE FOR MICHELINE

There's this old guy
who comes into the thrift store,
she tells me.
Buys suitcases.
That's it.
But lots of them.
More than you would need
to go somewhere.
He wears the same thing all the time anyway,
definitely doesn't need lots of bags.

She drinks her mocha
while chainsmoking,
but never stops
one bead after another
sliding onto the string.

Well, I asked around about him,
and they said
he fills them with poems.
Poems.
I was like,
how many fucking poems
could this guy have?

Her smoking-hand fingers hold a bead
that's carved like a skull.
The other hand vibrates so quickly
it looks like a timid lap dog.
But when the thread is close to the bead,
the hand calms and deftly enters
through the lower jaw
and exits through the top of the cranium.

So I thought I would tell you.
I thought since you like poetry,
you may want to know.
Anyway, it reminded me of you.

If I'm thinking of the right guy,
I told her, he could have that many poems.
He's a famous poet.
Kerouac did the Iintro to his first book.

If he's so famous,
she says defiantly,
what the fuck is he doing
wandering around Valencia Street
buying suitcases?
And can't he get someone
to wash his shirts for fuck's sake?

I have no answer for this.
I shrug my shoulders
and stare at her fingers.
Her hands are two black-nailed spiders,
methodically wrapping up prey.
She stops abruptly
and holds up the necklace.

You think someone would pay twenty bucks for this?

CRUMBLING CHICLETS

Broke a tooth flossing:
that's not good.
I recognized the sound of tooth hitting bathroom counter.
It's happened before.
It sounds like
when you throw a coke bottle
off a roof
in the dead of night.
There's that time pause
from that no-takebacks feeling
of the bottle flinging from the fingers
to the tinking pop when it hits the street.

It's the same pause
between the burning in your nose
and the beating of your heart

It's the same pause
between the sound of the lighter flicking
and the flame hitting the tin foil.

It's the same pause
between the lungs filling with the first inhale
and the brain lighting up.

It's the same pause
between saying I Love You
and hearing someone say it back

Back then, if you told me,
Meth will rot your teeth.
I would've told you
to rot in Hell.
I would've told you,
Fuck my teeth
and

Fuck you and fuck
the dentist you rode in on.

Two teeth gone recently —
this one about to go as well.

I'm lucky,
a lot of guys who did speed
have no teeth left.

I asked my dentist
what is it in meth that
crumbles the teeth,
ages them prematurely?

He says,
It's nothing in the meth,
it's that you guys
don't floss.

My dentist.
Always holding
the party line.

How I Made a Mortgage Loan Officer Cry or A Brief Recap of the Last 15 Years

And in 2040, she says,
you'll be all paid off.

I'll be dead by then,
I say.

She looks at me
like I just told her I have cancer.

I'm sorry, I tell her,
It's a little joke,
I know, you're 25 or something,
but once you pass 40
you can look downhill and see the bottom
It's not bad, it's okay.

That doesn't work any better,
I think she's crying a little.

There's only about fifteen years between us,
but it's the fifteen years
of ex girlfriends dying and
high school friends with grandchildren,
a bad back, gimpy knees, and failing eyesight.

At 25 I lived on Jim Beam, cigarettes, and sheer will,
I made all my choices based on the
line by the Butthole Surfers,
"It's better to regret something that you have done
than to regret something you haven't done."
learning my life skills from
Gibby Haynes wasn't a good idea,
but I trusted him more than I did my parents,
or teachers or cops.

I thought I was the next
Henry Rollins or Bukowski.
Any day it was only the next poem away,
that readers were going to figure me out.
That was supposed to fix me;
once my life was sold out spoken word shows
it would justify all the mistakes I'd made.

My first book was coming out.
I knew I just had to wait for everyone to read it,
the film rights to sell,
the big money advance for the next one,
everything would be okay.
I was going to be famous in Germany
and big in Japan,
hang out at the Chateau Marmont
with Johnny and Winona
and we'd all get real high,
and on the second day of the coke run
they'd say, You should write a
screenplay for us,
we're going to make a call.
And I'd play it cool,
say, No not me I'm a poet—
let them talk me into it.

I'd be interviewed by the *Paris Review*
and be *Rolling Stone*'s "Hot Poet to Watch,"
and when Sean Penn would ask me in
Interview Magazine
how I dealt with all the shit I'd been through,
I'd say,
Well Sean,
I guess all that shit
made me who I am.
Sometimes when life shits on you
you make yourself the nicest
shit-hat the world ever saw,

and you wear it like
it's Easter Fucking Sunday.

I'd be famous and it would feel like something,
anything different than what I felt like.
I wouldn't worry about money.
I'd buy an old warehouse,
fix it up and fill it with my friends,
and we'd just live there and be awesome together.
I thought it was coming.

The book came out
but it didn't fix anything
it didn't feel like anything
it was just a fucking book
so I drank more
and fucked more,
tried a few drugs I hadn't before.
I turned the music up louder.
I ran naked down the streets of common sense
waving a flag that said,
FUCK IT
I blamed everyone else for my failure
and fuck you especially if your book
did well, I hated you for it.

It worked really well
for seven bad years,
until it stopped working at all,
and then there were
funerals and stomach pains,
picking out yesterday's butts to smoke,
and crying in the light of stolen cable
when it was too late to call anyone.
At 32 I was near dead
and out of ideas.
I quit being such a hardass
quit blaming everyone else
and I did what humans are really good at:
waking up every day and fucking trying.

One little thing worked out
and I followed that with a bunch of others
until eight years later,
that loan officer
gives me the money
to get a tiny place of my own.
It's small with two bedrooms,
but it's mine and
it's bigger than any space I ever had to myself.

One way to look at it, I say,
is not that I'm buying a condo,
but that I'm buying a really awesome coffin.
I'm going to fill it with all of my favorite shit
and die in the middle of it like King Tut.

She didn't think that was funny either.

NEW WRITE BLOODY BOOKS FOR 2012

Strange Light
The *New York Times* says, "There's something that happens when you read Derrick Brown, a rekindling of faith in the weird, hilarious, shocking, beautiful power of words." This is the final collection from Derrick Brown, one of America's top-selling and touring poets. Everything hilarious and stirring is illuminated. The power of *Strange Light* is waiting.

Who Farted Wrong? Illustrated Weight Loss For the Mind
Syd Butler (of the sweet band, Les Savvy Fav) creates sketchy morsels to whet your appetite for wrong, and it will be delicious. There is no need to read between the lines of this new style of flash thinking speed illustration in this hilarious new book. Why? There are not that many lines.

New Shoes on a Dead Horse
The Romans believed that an artist's inspiration came from a spirit, called a genius, that lived in the walls of the artist's home. This character appears throughout Sierra DeMulder's book, providing charming commentary and biting insight on the young author's creative process and emotional path.

Good Grief
Elegantly-wrought misadventures as a freshly-graduated Michigan transplant, Stevie Edwards stumbles over foal legs through Chicago and kneels down to confront the wreckage of her skinned knees.

After the Witch Hunt
Megan Falley showcases her fresh, lucid poetry with a refreshing lack of jaded undertones. Armed with both humor and a brazen darkness, each poem in this book is another swing of the pick axe in this young woman's tunnel, insistent upon light.

I Love Science!
Humorous and thought provoking, Shanney Jean Maney's book effortlessly combines subjects that have previously been thought too diverse to have anything in common. Science, poetry and Jeff Goldblum form covalent bonds that put the poetic fire underneath our bunsen burners. A Lab Tech of words, Maney turns language into curious, knowledge-hungry poetry. Foreword by Lynda Barry.

Time Bomb Snooze Alarm
Bucky Sinister, a veteran poet of the working class, layers his gritty truths with street punk humor. A menagerie of strange people and stranger moments that linger in the dark hallway of Sinister's life. Foreword by Randy Blythe of "Lamb of God".

News Clips and Ego Trips
A collection of helpful articles from *Next...* magazine, which gave birth to the Southern California and national poetry scene in the mid-'90s. It covers the growth of spoken word, page poetry and slam, with interviews and profiles of many poets and literary giants like Patricia Smith, Henry Rollins and Miranda July. Edited by G. Murray Thomas.

Slow Dance With Sasquatch
Jeremy Radin invites you into his private ballroom for a waltz through the forest at the center of life, where loneliness and longing seamlessly shift into imagination and humor.

The Smell of Good Mud
Queer parenting in conservative Oklahoma, Lauren Zuniga finds humor and beauty in this collection of new poems. This explores the grit and splendor of collective living, and other radical choices. It is a field guide to blisters and curtsies.

OTHER WRITE BLOODY BOOKS (2003 - 2011)

Great Balls of Flowers (2009)
Steve Abee's poetry is accessible, insightful, hilarious, compelling,
upsetting, and inspiring. TNB Book of the Year.

Everything Is Everything (2010)
The latest collection from poet Cristin O'Keefe Aptowicz,
filled with crack squirrels, fat presidents, and el Chupacabra.

Working Class Represent (2011)
A young poet humorously balances an office job with the life
of a touring performance poet in Cristin O'Keefe Aptowicz's third book of poetry

Oh, Terrible Youth (2011)
Cristin O'Keefe Aptowicz's plump collection commiserates and celebrates
all the wonder, terror, banality and comedy that is the long journey to adulthood.

Hot Teen Slut (2011)
Cristin O'Keefe Aptowicz's second book recounts stories of
a virgin poet who spent a year writing for the porn business.

Dear Future Boyfriend (2011)
Cristin O'Keefe Aptowicz's debut collection of poetry tackles
love and heartbreak with no-nonsense honesty and wit.

38 Bar Blues (2011)
C. R. Avery's second book, loaded with bar-stool musicality and brass-knuckle poetry.

Catacomb Confetti (2010)
Inspired by nameless Parisian skulls in the catacombs of France,
Catacomb Confetti assures Joshua Boyd's poetic immortality.

Born in the Year of the Butterfly Knife (2004)
The Derrick Brown poetry collection that birthed Write Bloody Publishing.
Sincere, twisted, and violently romantic.

I Love You Is Back (2006)
A poetry collection by Derrick Brown.
"One moment tender, funny, or romantic, the next, visceral, ironic,
and revelatory—Here is the full chaos of life." (Janet Fitch, *White Oleander*)

Scandalabra (2009)
Former paratrooper Derrick Brown releases a stunning collection of poems written
at sea and in Nashville, TN. About.com's book of the year for poetry.

Workin' Mime to Five (2011)
Dick Richards is a fired cruise ship pantomimist. You too can learn
his secret, creative pantomime moves. Humor by Derrick Brown.

Don't Smell the Floss (2009)
Award-winning writer Matty Byloos' first book of bizarre, absurd, and deliciously
perverse short stories puts your drunk uncle to shame.

Reasons to Leave the Slaughter (2011)
Ben Clark's book of poetry revels in youthful discovery from the heartland
and the balance between beauty and brutality.

Over the Anvil We Stretch (2008)
2-time poetry slam champ Anis Mojgani's first collection: a Pushcart-Nominated
batch of backwood poetics, Southern myth, and rich imagery.

The Feather Room (2011)
Anis Mojgani's second collection of poetry explores storytelling and
poetic form while traveling farther down the path of magic realism.

Animal Ballistics (2009)
Trading addiction and grief for empowerment and humor with her poetry,
Sarah Morgan does it best.

Rise of the Trust Fall (2010)
Award-winning feminist poet Mindy Nettifee
releases her second book of funny, daring, gorgeous, accessible poems.

Love in a Time of Robot Apocalypse (2011)
Latino-American poet David Perez releases his first book
of incisive, arresting, and end-of-the-world-as-we-know-it poetry.

No More Poems About the Moon (2008)
A pixilated, poetic and joyful view of a hyper-sexualized,
wholeheartedly confused, weird, and wild America with Michael Roberts.

The New Clean (2011)
Jon Sands' poetry redefines what it means to laugh, cry, mop it up and start again.

Miles of Hallelujah (2010)
Slam poet/pop-culture enthusiast Rob "Ratpack Slim" Sturma
shows first collection of quirky, fantastic, romantic poetry.

Sunset at the Temple of Olives (2011)
Paul Suntup's unforgettable voice merges subversive surrealism
and vivid grief in this debut collection of poetry.

Spiking the Sucker Punch (2009)
Nerd heartthrob, award-winning artist and performance poet,
Robbie Q. Telfer stabs your sensitive parts with his wit-dagger.

Racing Hummingbirds (2010)
Poet/performer Jeanann Verlee releases an award-winning book
of expertly crafted, startlingly honest, skin-kicking poems.

Live for a Living (2007)
Acclaimed performance poet Buddy Wakefield releases his second collection
about healing and charging into life face first.

Gentleman Practice (2011)
Righteous Babe Records artist and 3-time International Poetry Champ
Buddy Wakefield spins a nonfiction tale of a relay race to the light.

How to Seduce a White Boy in Ten Easy Steps (2011)
Debut collection for feminist, biracial poet Laura Yes Yes
dazzles with its explorations into the politics and metaphysics of identity.

WRITE BLOODY ANTHOLOGIES

The Elephant Engine High Dive Revival (2009)
Our largest tour anthology ever! Features unpublished work by
Buddy Wakefield, Derrick Brown, Anis Mojgani and Shira Erlichman!

The Good Things About America (2009)
American poets team up with illustrators to recognize the beauty and wonder in our
nation. Various authors. Edited by Kevin Staniec and Derrick Brown

Junkyard Ghost Revival (2008)
Tour anthology of poets, teaming up for a journey of the US in a small van.
Heart-charging, socially active verse.

The Last American Valentine:
Illustrated Poems To Seduce And Destroy (2008)
Acclaimed authors including Jack Hirschman, Beau Sia, Jeffrey McDaniel,
Michael McClure, Mindy Nettifee and more. 24 authors and 12 illustrators
team up for a collection of non-sappy love poetry. Edited by Derrick Brown

Learn Then Burn (2010)
Exciting classroom-ready anthology for introducing new writers
to the powerful world of poetry. Edited by Tim Stafford and Derrick Brown.

Learn Then Burn Teacher's Manual (2010)
Tim Stafford and Molly Meacham's turn key classroom-safe guide
to accompany *Learn Then Burn*: A modern poetry anthology for the classroom.

Knocking at the Door: Poems for Approaching the Other (2011)
An exciting compilation of diverse authors that explores the concept of the Other
from all angles. Innovative writing from emerging and established poets.

WWW.WRITEBLOODY.COM

Pull Your Books Up
By Their Bootstraps

WRITEBLOODY
QUALITY AMERICAN BOOKS

Write Bloody Publishing distributes and promotes great books of fiction, poetry and art every year. We are an independent press dedicated to quality literature and book design, with an office in Long Beach, CA.

Our employees are authors and artists so we call ourselves a family. Our design team comes from all over America: modern painters, photographers and rock album designers create book covers we're proud to be judged by.

We publish and promote 8-12 tour-savvy authors per year. We are grass-roots, D.I.Y., bootstrap believers. Pull up a good book and join the family. Support independent authors, artists and presses.

Visit us online:

WRITEBLOODY.COM

CPSIA information can be obtained at www.ICGtesting.com
Printed in the USA
LVOW041127220712

290996LV00005B/2/P